Crying of Small Motors

poems

Craig Brandis

Finishing Line Press
Georgetown, Kentucky

Crying of Small Motors

Publisher: Leah Huete de Maines
Editor: Christen Kincaid
Cover Art: Alamy Photos
Author Photo: Carol Brandis
Cover Design: Craig Brandis

Order online: www.finishinglinepress.com
          also available on amazon.com

Author inquiries and mail orders:
Finishing Line Press
PO Box 1626
Georgetown, Kentucky 40324
USA

Contents

WORK ROOM
Cat Scan 1
How Life After Returning Home Makes You Up 2
Road Work 3
First Christmas 5
Body Retrieval 6
Last Office 7
Live Birth 8

CAMP
Operating Room 11
Rose of Sharon 12
Berlin Wall 13
Aftermath 14
Crying of Small Motors 15
Parma Idaho 16
Wire Sparrow 17
Fin and Rib 18

CONCRETE STARSHIP
Your Kisses 25
Army Medic 26
Concrete Starship 27
One Hundred Thousand Miles 28
Wormwood 29
Portland Jury Duty #4 30
On Self Portrait by Ukrainian Artist Yana Movchan ... 31
Sea Lion 32
Monocle 33
East of Here 34
Care of Memories 35
Gentians on the Water's Face 36
Tumblehome 37
Crossing the Mountains in Winter 38
I Like It When You Say Don't Do That 39

Acknowledgments 41
About the Author 43

For Carol, Joel and Jenna

WORK ROOM

CAT Scan

of my skull in the surgeon's office
like a Da Vinci post-mortem
a putty of shades
smeared by movement
in the brrr-ing machine
Newly pendulumlike
about multiple axes
as if a friend had sent
a funny birthday card
with a tilt-a-whirl
holographic skull
of a chimpanzee
front teeth protruding
lips blown out like someone
in a fool's rage over
missed chances—
now I am bent over
under the weight of this
bloody hind quarter
in a slurry of guilt
rain and Glenlivet
The elk had run injured
had needed two shots
the truck still a half mile
and a creek crossing away
My feet like dead cod
I am losing my grip this
blood-slick carcass and all
the punk stars with long
sleeves of lime curd
dragging their chains over
and up the long hill

How Life After Returning Home Makes You Up

Like bears swatting
at fish, kids outside
hit tennis balls
against your western
wall. Soon you are a
swimming pool
built in memory
of fallen soldiers.
Decent clouds
come and go. You let
teenagers slip into
your mercury-blue
water to fan and flex.
Lifeguards with boat rope
shoulders. Think of hair
burning—that scorched boot
smell in the seconds
before skin knows
what happens next.

Road Work

She's leaking hydraulic, he says
as he lowers the blade of his
D8 dozer to the ground,
shuts it down. The smell of newly
exposed forest soil mixes
with diesel exhaust.
Robins drop from the
trees to gorge on a sudden
bloom of nightcrawlers.
There is a boulder in the road
bed he needs to dynamite
anyway. He can replace the
broken hose later.
Jumping down from the track,
he sees a startling blue
eggshell in the gravel at the edge
of the cut bank. He drills an eighteen
inch hole in the boulder, gently
packs it with a full stick,
back fills with gravel. Runs the
wires two hundred feet back.
Yells for everyone to stay clear:

Fire in the hole!

He touches the wires to an
old truck battery. When the
deep thud hits his chest he
stands still, looking straight
up for falling rocks—
every other time
but this one.
sky
yelling in

his sleeve
falling from
the upstairs

window when
he was six
an upturned root
ball—his mother
her own
hoard of stones

someone with
acetylene breath
leaning over him
ribs snapping
left leg-mind on fire

First Christmas

Now a man sees a
box of outdoor lights
thinks those need me.
Two wicker deer
in the basement
with animatronic ears,
shoulders turning.
Neighbor is always
too cheerful for me
says driveway things
I don't encumber.
TV snout calls me
inside, it is getting
late dinner doesn't
make itself, how I think
about your pinewood feet,
the keening they said
wasn't really you.
It is a line of credit with
a beast for collateral.
As muslin frays
over cheekbones,
I try to keep it in view,
put my hands on the places
where others became
weathered gifts without
looking around too much
to land sputter-blind
in the narrow sunshine,
scattered and piecewise,
more catchall than curtain.

Body Retrieval

The girl's body is stuck under
a ledge at the bottom of a plunge pool
where the river spins like a mad cyclone
bent on boring to the earth's center.
His only tool, a long pole, it takes
him a full day to get to her, tie the
retrieval ropes and lever her out.
Quiet as eels, people stand and watch.
He brings her up, lays her on a sandbar.
At the parking lot, people try to offer him money.
He drives home. Bone-deep headache. In rough
sleep he sees the frozen knobs of her hands.
The outhouse at his church youth camp.
Through the chink, a yolk of light, then nothing.
His parent's farm. A Berkshire hog with
bloodshot eyes in a field of stumps.
Butchering day. Long skein of intestines.
Head with hairy nostrils set aside for cheese.
Steady drip of blood. Dogs baying for scraps.
Marsh lights in the summer darkness.

Last Office

My dad, so sick with pancreatic cancer
he looked like a desiccated insect in amber,
insisted on going every day to his part time
job as chaplain in a halfway house for
recovering addicts and offenders. I only
saw him cry when we told him it was time
to stop working, close his tiny windowless
office and come home. That night, he rolled
out a long piece of butcher paper on the
dining room table. Next day I found, in
shaky letters, his design for his tombstone:
Rev. E. L. Brandis, Army and VA Chaplain

Live Birth

Diego Rivera said, to make a mural come alive, he
mixed in some death. I nod, smell the stone dust

of the Anaconda mine, listen to a five-story loader growl
under heavy lidded eyes. Yesterday, I watched a seal

swing a salmon in its mouth, a blood-lined purse spraying
coins over silvered wood—a security guard on swing shift

in Fukushima absorbing his last dose of radiation. I want
to speak of things that argue under bridges before the light

can fix them. Use everything, put it all in. I walk past the
middle school, scuffling my feet in a drift of winter road

salt the sweeper missed. When Willow was born with
a bowel obstruction and needed immediate surgery,

staff, sharp and friendly as pins, didn't blink. That's what
I think of when I think of being born—wounded in

the stomach, a blue quickening by the window, the world's
bloody cord. Light incoming like a thicket of arrows.

CAMP

Operating Room

is full of oddities

a plastic stork   blue

tube grass   a synthetic sun under

a cumbrous umbrella

red-bearded guy

calls himself a gas passer

bossa nova music

white gravy   in the back of my hand

beneath the rim of the caldera

only what is fibrous or damned

skin of dark salt

arm sockets popping like kelp balls

sticking out of my side

the gutter of a house

Rose of Sharon

"I charge you...that you stir not up"
　　　　　—Rose of Sharon, Sacred Harp Hymnal #254

I am in a dying
marriage trying
to sing my way out
of it in a country
church in Alabama.
An inchworm
measuring the
length of kingdoms
with my body.
When falling
through them,
the ice rings
of Saturn are
barely there.

Berlin Wall

Statues in the Tiergarten stand like
Olympic wrestlers under mineral

sedation. An oily fug of coal smoke
blankets the city. The Reichstag building

looks like it eats butterflies. Lunch in
the student union building—a bowl

of heavy broth with a fist-sized dough ball.
Frau Hauer, an elderly widow, collects string,

cleans bathrooms in return for rent, remembers
starvation in the streets. She says softly,

"you didn't have much bombing in America?"
Two people try to escape to the West by

swimming the Wannsee at night from East
Berlin. They don't make it. Honeyed tea

in porcelain cups. Ceramic coal ovens
stand in the corner of living rooms like

glass blue soldiers. Another entire city waits
beneath the streets, breathing through straws.

Aftermath

A shadow props up
the gutted warehouse
where we spent the
night. To be keen all
the time—not to swerve.
Ten minutes out of every
hour is enough most days.
A man with boulders in his
soul, a dock holding onto
its string of boat horses,
a bone-drenched woman
with praise for a God who
is stealthy, a barn cat.
Out on the freeway—
silence. As if someone had
snagged every sound from
a skiff with a pruning hook
and put it in a sack.

Crying of Small Motors

I just want to go home,
she said, before her
breath became hoarse.
Wheezy. Vacant.
Later there will be glue
for eyes, a small knot
of sensible, dark haired
music. He tried to retrieve
her wedding ring, wincing
at the snap. Picked out
burial clothes, earrings,
strands of costume
pearls, underwear, bra.
Driving with the window
down. The radio's burr
over the neighborhood
crying of small motors
and the tight-lipped
jurists of honeybees.

Parma Idaho

Mounds of sugar beets under
halogen, marooned in pressure
waves like fossil dinosaur turds.

Lurid thunder eggs. And
always the two Lebanese
brothers who walk and argue.

A six-year-old boy drowned in an
irrigation ditch. His father a tethered
dirigible in white Adidas.

Church is headstones in hill rows
wearing an unrelenting east
wind. Pacific as cheatgrass.

It's not personal when someone leaves, though
they try to make it so, rumbling like a John
Deere tractor with a bored aneurysm.

Wire Sparrow

When my high school friend Jim was killed in a vintage
biplane crash, they held an open casket service. That bothered
even my father, a WWII veteran. He was busted up pretty bad,
Dad said, with a tight lip.

I was terrified to look. Jim was the first dead person I'd
seen. He looked like a painted wax figurine of the boy
I knew—left in the sun too long. He had been pretty
from the ground though as he climbed into the summer
morning sky over Pearson air park in his canvas and wire
starship. Making necks sore from looking up. Those
impossibly slow turns on swoopy putt-putt wings.

Uneasy jam of witnesses. Sour smell of spilled fuel.
Running. Wreckage. Cars starting to pull away with kids stuck
to their seats. Looking out the side windows like toy raccoons.

I hid my grief inside for years like a ruined animal. No one
seemed to talk about what happened. One day twenty years
later while visiting our old church, I happened to stand on the
spot near the entrance where Jim had been. The organist was
practicing before the service—His Eye is on the Sparrow.
I broke down. Jim's mother was there that morning.
She spotted me. I know, she said. Together, we poured
out our sorrow like galled wine.

When we carry grief with us, pushing it ahead on a small
cart, the dead can't say no—so they say nothing. Rumbly
church organ. The smell of worn-out carpet. Sunday hats
with organdy gauze. Outside, the sky's pinned-on shirt with
a folded meadow pond over the pocket.

Fin and Rib

The sun walked down the mountain faster
than I could cross the river.

•

I have been writing with such a small part of my mind.
I poisoned the ants good.

•

Stillborn and unappeasable gods. It's alright
if you sleep alone.

•

A kiss of blind tape where the two ends meet.

•

Jonah in the fin and rib of things.

•

At the National Art museum. Everything isn't in there.

•

A startled elk explodes the aspen trees.

•

We found him dead in a blue fog of hospital.

•

A tray of chiles. Their small-town ways.

•

My words swirled like dirty water in a can.

•

A bus with bug-eyes and high-waisted pants.

•

Dangers of surviving are never explained.

•

Molten solitude in island colors.

•

Ceiling, put away your sad face. Tell me what you saw.

•

Under the apple trees, a drift of wild asparagus.

•

In a body cast, I stank like the town dump.

•

Himalayan moon the color of a calf's ear.

•

Sorrows, poetry.
Ouzo, bouzouki.

•

Like tinned trout with dill—little poem,
where's your pull tab?

•

Silence was stacked beside the fields like pipe
after wheel irrigation is done.

•

A ballistic missile can calculate how much time
you have to wipe yourself.

•

Winter's blunt nose pulled me in.

•

On a day like brocaded glass, it all fell away.

•

Betrayed by fiat currency we drank
from each other's mouths.

•

Nansen drifting north with the ice.
Chthonic darkness.

•

Trees underwater for millennia.
Witness protection.

•

Granddaughter paints leopard spots
on the moon. How gently time collapses.

•

Carpathia steams towards Titanic. Deck chairs aligned.
Funnels brave.

•

They carried their houses up a long hill.
Saying yes, saying no.

CONCRETE STARSHIP

Your Kisses
(for Carol)

A rave in Berlin.
Carnival in a village
in Trinidad. The
aurora borealis
in a martini glass.
An electric cannibal
floor show. Marlene
Dietrich wearing khakis
at the western front.
Coho salmon running
in glitter pants. Bogart
and Bacall on a sailboat
off Catalina Island.
A slow drive down
the Brittany coast. A
Tasmanian drug lord.

Army Medic

His spine runs on
bourbon, spite and
green ice. Gagging on
an apple, each departing
soul a sparse tent of oxygen,
a bale of farther food
moving like sea in a jar.
If he could melt the maze
of tongues, shove away
the bible, daisies, wave
off the transfer tube
before the knees buckle,
he might be known as
a purifier. Back and
forth like a trembling
crow he marks the spot
where the air rudder goes,
until she gasps, circles back,
a fermata in a wheelchair.
Army wraparound shades
propped up—blind as
grandmother on
a snowy evening
behind the leather
padded doors of
the US capitol.

Concrete Starship

We worked on a section of the new bridge
to give back shadows to the river.

I remember the first time I walked the span, looking
straight down on Canada geese flying above the water.
I was lucky to get hired as a day laborer right out of high
school. One morning the ground fog so thick you could
not see the river—the bridge rose like a concrete starship
built by backwards men. Compound curves the whole
way, twisting around three axes, swerving three hundred
and ten feet sideways as it crosses—soil problems.

The northern abutments flare at the top like Frank Lloyd
Wright's tapered tree columns in the Johnson wax
building, descending like sky grown redwoods to land in a
neighborhood of small cottages built for papermill workers.

No superstructure over the roadbed—a pure ribbon.
We knew it would be possible to flip a car off the side, but
the angle and momentum would have to be perfect. A year
after it opened, on a glove-soft summer night, it came—
the rare shadow that leaves a mark on the water.

One Hundred Thousand Miles

Southern Idaho. Endless alkali desert like bands of old paint
scraped on the land with a putty knife. Hours in the car listening
to a single radio station from Pocatello— crop prices, country
and southern rock, high school football, as the Teton mountains'
big red shoulders rise from a ruff of quaking aspen. They guard
the gates of my earliest sense of what home is—a place of love,
loss and letting go. I'm here to see Wyoming one last time while
my ailing father is still alive.

Dad was chaplain at the VA hospital in Sheridan. He was also
a circuit preacher and drove long distances to hold services in
Shell, Ten Sleep, Story and other small towns in northern
Wyoming. Once he drove to Story to conduct a funeral for
a rancher who had died in an accident. Before the service,
the man's wife came up to him carrying a pair of cowboy
boots. She asked him if she could put them on her dead
husband. When he asked why, she said: where he is going,
he will need them. The look in her eye told him she wasn't
looking for a laugh or sympathy, just some neighborly assistance.

The funeral home where they turned my father's body back into
dust is now a Portland brew pub. I had a beer there on his
birthday. Listening to the thwhirr of traffic outside, I remembered
his wry smile—he would have enjoyed the irony. Dad didn't drink.
Driving home, the tire slap on the pavement reminded me of the
thousands of miles we drove in his 1957 Volkswagen bus—a sheet
metal Galapagos turtle with a broken heater. Snow fences tilted
at crazy angles. Wind-shivered Conoco signs.

Wormwood

Heart, you
rib-nailed

kalimba
overlooking

the great city,
what if I took

you to a different
town where they

love the side wound
more than the cross—

would you gallop
back to cut

out the piece
that displeases?

Portland Jury Duty #4

police photos showed
puffy red face and ears / car

                              keys thrown out the window
                                 yea i smacked her he said
                                 like i do every day / i even
                                            spit on her
                                 the people of Portland

are evil i'd like to stab them
all in the neck
watch them bleed out

                              or go down to hell / get some
                                 demons to come back

                and help me
maybe i'm like you
maybe i'm one of
those cardboard

                                    cutouts like the
                              display in Burger King
                                 where Whoppers
                                    are all in all

                        i could
make
you one

On Self Portrait by Ukrainian Artist Yana Movchan

a pink camelia / pinned next to a pale /
buttoned collar with / long thin points /

tucked into her coat pocket /
a red sprig / like brain capillaries /

like Mary / she holds /
her hushed / octopus-arms close /

over her shoulders / saints
glow-wander /

break loose in a /
north-by-northeast wind /

gazing between the icons /
she locks her lichen /
eyes on you /

In Kyiv is /
a terrible longing /
interminable /

in its freshness /
like the inner bark /
of trees

Sea Lion

How sharper than a serpent's tooth it is
To have a thankless child!
                    —King Lear, Act 1, Scene 4

Her great boulder head surfaces
mid-river, blowing and snorting from
from bottomless nostrils like bore holes
in basalt. She stares at me in my paper-thin
rowing shell for a defiant minute,
a slick yard of Coho draped silver-red
in her mouth. Later, as I turn and pull for
the boathouse, the water behind me explodes.
She hunts with a ferocity, which seems overkill,
at first. At fourteen, I watched my father open
his mother's will. There were old wounds
between them no tourniquet of years
could bind up or heal. A pale check slid
out of the folded papers and fluttered
to the floor. It was made out to him,
in low angular letters like sharp-chinned
soldiers, in the amount of one dollar. I
see her sitting on her screened porch in
Richmond. Counterpane, black tea, bible.
A serpent's tooth—her calcareous loss.

Monocle
(for Joel)

The money is soft in the sea
Where I stopped and you went on.

I have been writing like a man
Angry, helmeted, on his back.

Wandering like Cretans—
My rain-thick shades.

East of Here
(after Tranströmer)

Power lines—
long distance
runners across
brown hills.
Above the
small print
grasses, a horse's
double field
of vision folds
the country
lengthwise.

Care of Memories

Piles of paper,
scraps like herds
of tiny cattle
milling around.
You ask if I am
speaking
as if the shower
was running
and I should
check on it,
as if the dog was
making that
choking sound.

Gentians on the Water's Face

This is the part the messenger plays
    Getting the old wax tyrant to smile
There are gentians on the water's face
    That's her on the left in the green raincoat
Where airplanes fashion the thought of themselves
    Imagine you are the one being clarified
Because my task is to stroll a bit farther
    Beads of sweat, molecules of thought
On days when we picked Italian plums
    The loading dock where things are pulled apart
And the bridges stood tall in their wizardry
    It was late or at least the early part of late
Revealed far from the old countries
    It's different now—the edges look stiffer
An aluminum snake no closer than this
    Cadmium blue, wasn't it, or maybe a shade darker?

Tumblehome

(for Jenna)

nobody's / mesmer-eyes / bent leg / small wag/
whip taut / in a kill shelter / in Oklahoma /
until she / found him / brought him /
home / named him Phantom /

Crossing the Mountains in Winter

I'm driving east from Seattle over Stevens Pass.
Just past the summit ski area, the road enters
a canyon of ice. Plows like mechanical buffalo
have gnawed the snow back to the guardrails.
Above them, rows of blue-black fir trees, droopy
in white epaulets. Beyond these are range after
range of snowy mountain peaks gouged by valleys
where black bears fatten on huckleberries in the fall,
porcupines wander in magnificent indifference,
gray wolves, lynx, and wolverine hunt. And not that
long ago, the California condor—a bird with a
nine-foot wingspan that inspired the legend of the
thunderbird, picked over the bones of their kills.

Hours later, as I turn into the Wenatchee River
canyon, I see a family of deer in my lane. No
chance to swerve—I hit them at forty-five miles
an hour. Head. Hooves. Windshield. Tessellated
glass. Brown fur mixed with green silage.

My ears buzz. Seeming hours go by. Finally, a
state patrol car pulls over. Then a man in a pickup
stops. He walks over. Kills the injured deer with
a tire iron. Lifts them into the back of his somewhat
gray truck brindled with body repairs that still need
paint. Sound of wipers batting at cottoned snow.

He says he hunts here in the fall. Was on his way
to a job interview at the Chief Joseph dam.
His left eyelid droops, like a sash window in a
dwelling someone lives in only part of the year.
Sour tobacco breath. Red and blue patrol lights
flutter across his face. Deer come down from
the hills in winter, cross the highway to get to water,
he says. Shocked meat tastes okay if you hang it quick.
I nod as if I know this to be true. He wipes deer blood
and browse off his jacket with a gas station rag. Like
inverted land, the backs of his hands. Blue spider rivers.
Bony leather like old kills. Road signs with bullet acne.

I Like It When You Say Don't Do That

Given how ordinary isn't feeling well
  The smelting process you counted on doesn't work
And I won't say how much it offends me
  His wife left him after triple dog years
The bunches of dried gunk on the stairs
  A dreadful science that works
How crabapples rot before they ripen
  To that burr hole behind the eyes I say
You tell me I think too much
  From the court of no appeal
I'm trying out a way to say I love you that sits on the stairs
  They made it as far as the orchard
I'm working on a building like the early Christians
  Better after it fell in
Mine is made of blue mud and marsh straw
  Breaking the windshield of everything small
How could I do it any differently
  Hard to see it along the fence line
You take infinite care with light construction
  Our low ceiling of acanthus leaves
And I want to tell you how much I like it
  When you say don't do that

Acknowledgments

I am grateful to the editors of the following publications in which these poems, sometimes in a different form, first appeared:

Oxford Magazine: Army Medic

Parhelion Literary Magazine: Live Birth, First Christmas, I Like it When You Say Don't Do That, Sea Lion, Last Office, Operating Room, Berlin Wall, Concrete Starship

Trampoline: Cat Scan, First Light, Body Retrieval, How Life After Returning Home Makes You Up

The American Journal of Poetry: Rose of Sharon, Monocle

Work Literary Magazine: Road Work

The Café Review: Tumblehome

Streetlight Magazine: Parma Idaho

Clementine Unbound: Aftermath

Thank you to my teachers at the Attic Institute of Arts and Letters: David Biespiel, Matthew Dickman, Ashley Toliver and Ed Skoog. They gave me the confidence to swing for the fences, embrace revision and to be in it for the long haul. Thanks also to Ines P. Rivera Prosdocimi for her meticulous reading and suggestions. Monica Youn helped me improve my work with her laser-eyed insights. My friend Anne Griffin, the poet-mavin of first reads, gets grateful applause here too. Special thanks to my wife Carol for her close reading, good humor and unwavering support.

Craig Brandis lives in Lake Oswego, Oregon with his wife Carol. He worked as a carpenter, woodworker, field engineer, surveyor, and landscape designer before pursuing a graduate degree in computer science and a career in software development, training and product management. He holds multiple patents for smartphone methods and systems. A lifelong student, he studies poetry at the Attic Institute of Arts and Letters in Portland, Oregon and is a multi-year member of its Poet's Studio. His poems and reviews have been published in *Oxford Magazine, Palette Poetry, Parhelion, Trampoline, American Journal of Poetry, Poetry Quarterly, The Café Review, Streetlight Magazine* and elsewhere. He was a semi-finalist for the 2022 Berkshire prize for a first or second book and for the 2022 Sally Albiso prize.